Values in the
Classroom

Published by
Charles E. Merrill Publishing Company
A Bell & Howell Company
Columbus, Ohio 43216

This book was set in Souvenir and Optima.
The production editor was Frances Margolin.
The cover was prepared by Will Chenoweth.

International Standard Book Number:
0-675-08513-6

Library of Congress Catalog Card Number:
76-52864

1   2   3   4   5   6   81   80   79   78   77

Printed in the United States of America

Values in the Classroom

Cara B. Volkmor
California Regional Resource Center,
University of Southern California

Anne Langstaff Pasanella
California Regional Resource Center,
University of Southern California

Louis E. Raths
State University of New York, Fredonia

Charles E. Merrill Publishing Company
A Bell & Howell Company
Columbus   London   Toronto   Sydney

ACKNOWLEDGMENTS

Each of the following persons made a personal and unique contribution to the production of this program, and we take this opportunity to say a special thank you to:

Bob and Leslie Galeotti,
  Galeotti Graphics, Ontario, Ca.
Judy Grayson, formerly of
  Duarte Unified School District, Duarte, Ca.
Dodie Leonard and her students from
  Royal Oaks School, Duarte.
Phyllis Olivos and her students from
  Royal Oaks School, Duarte.
Vic Schneidman and his students from
  Andres Duarte Middle School.
Alice Smith and her students from
  Valley View School, Duarte.
Sandy Zygielbaum and her students from
  Maxwell School, Duarte.
The Jacobs Family, La Crescenta, Ca.
Helen Langstaff and Jeannie Tavlin,
  Los Angeles Unified Schools District, Los Angeles, Ca.

Marlene Weston
   Placentia Unified School District, Placentia, Ca.
Tim Williams, Photographer
                    and to
Les March,
   California State University, Fullerton, Ca., our valued friend who
   developed most of the activities for modules 3, 4, and 5.

CONTENTS

to our families
  Bill and David
  Joe, Laurie, Doug, and David

Values in the
Classroom

Introduction

This program is about valuing—the process by which we acquire, use, and modify the behavioral guides which shape our experiences, and therefore our lives. It outlines a theory of values and illustrates various methods which children and adults can use in the clarification of their values. This program is based on the assumption that *values and valuing are uniquely personal dimensions* of the human experience; therefore, the program itself does not suggest particular values which should be taught, or acquired at specific ages, nor does it attempt to provide a curriculum for values education. Instead, it attempts to show adults how to identify, confront, get close to, and act upon whatever is of value to them, so that they can facilitate the process of valuing in their classrooms with each individual student. This program will interest all who are concerned with helping people become more purposeful, more productive, more enthusiastic, more able to cope effectively with the environment, and more aware of who they really are. It is an open-ended program; the results cannot be guaranteed, because they depend upon trust and faith in the magnificent potential of all human beings.

VALUES CLARIFICATION: SOME PERSPECTIVE

The term *values clarification* was first introduced by Louis Raths in the late fifties when he taught at New York University. Since that time, books, articles, exercises, materials, and programs about values clarification have proliferated. A sampling is listed at the end of this book. In general, the values clarification approach, as it has been expressed, expanded, and interpreted by various authors, focuses on sensitizing people to values and increasing critical thinking and feeling about issues, while emphasizing freedom of choice, independent decision making, and a call to action. Imparting particular beliefs, response modes, or values is antithetical to the values clarification method.

Each person should draw values clarification activities from his or her personal experience with life. These activities can be used to help us deal with the conflicts and confusions so characteristic of our lives in an age of accelerated change.

Take a moment to consider the following values dilemma.

Suppose you are a government decision maker in Washington, D.C., when World War III breaks out.

A fallout shelter under your administration in a remote Montana highland contains only enough space, air, food and water for six people for three months, but ten people wish to be admitted.

The ten have agreed by radio contact that for the survival of the human race you must decide which six of them shall be saved. You have exactly thirty minutes to make up your mind before Washington goes up in smoke. These are your choices:

    1. A 16-year-old girl of questionable IQ, a high-school dropout, pregnant.

    2. A policeman with a gun (which cannot be taken from him), thrown off the force recently for brutality.

    3. A clergyman, 75.

    4. A woman physician, 36, known to be a confirmed racist.

    5. A male violinist, 46, who served seven years for pushing narcotics.

    6. A 20-year-old black militant, no special skills.

    7. A former prostitute, female, 39.

    8. An architect, a male homosexual.

    9. A 26-year-old law student.

    10. The law student's 25-year-old wife who spent the last nine months in a mental hospital, still heavily sedated. They refuse to be separated (Simon, 1972, p. 00).

Figuring out your choices—and how you arrived at them—is values clarification. . . . Suppose that the minister is 40 instead of 75—and is female; the architect is heterosexual; the black militant is a biochemist; and the policeman has just won a community relations award.

Who then?

In contrast to values clarification is the cognitive-developmental approach to moral education advanced by Lawrence Kohlberg. According to Kohlberg, there are six defined moral stages, logically ordered, which comprise an analytical model. He emphasizes the cognitive processes in making moral decisions with little regard for the role of emotions. Kohlberg claims to have validated the six stages through longitudinal and cross-cultural studies. References to the work of Kohlberg and his colleagues are also included at the end of this book.

As you work through the six modules of this program, *our* values about valuing and teaching will be evident. We believe that:

1.   It is the school's responsibility to teach children about the _process_ of valuing.

2.   Self-respect is critical; every child needs to see himself or herself as important and unique.

3.   We all need to be aware of and tolerant of values which differ from our own and know what we value and why.

4.   The teacher's role is to provide structure for the value-clarifying process, supply materials, schedule time for values clarification activities, and facilitate interaction.

5.   While values education has recently received increased attention from educators, there remains much to be done to make it an integral, continuing, and living part of the curriculum.

DESCRIPTION OF THIS PROGRAM

The entire program is based on the work of Louis Raths and his colleagues Merrill Harmin and Sidney Simon. There are six modules; each module consists of a MEDIAPAK audio-visual component and a corresponding book chapter. The six modules are:

1.   The Process of Valuing: A Point of View
2.   Values: Saying Who You Are
3.   Values Clarification Methods: Written Activities
4.   Values Clarification Methods: The Clarifying Response
5.   Values Clarification Methods: Discussion Activities
6.   Taking a New Road: Getting Started—Keeping Going

Each chapter in this book is articulated with sections of the text *Values and Teaching* (Raths, Harmin, and Simon, 1966, 1977). In each chapter, specific learner objectives are stated and the MEDIAPAK content is reviewed and extended. Many activities are included throughout the book to provide you with the opportunity to practice and experience values clarification methods. These activities can be adapted for later use with students of various ages.

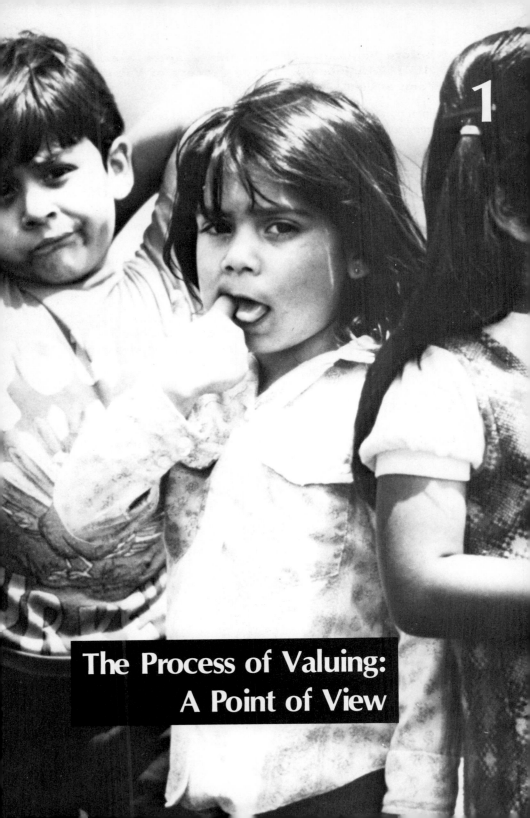

The Process of Valuing:
A Point of View

1

Before beginning to read this chapter, view the MEDIAPAK labeled "1, The Process of Valuing: A Point of View."

When you have completed both the media and print portions of this module, you will be able to:

1. *Define the term "valuing" as it is used in this program.*

2. *Specify the five requirements or criteria of a "value."*

3. *List at least four categories of "value indicators," and write two examples of each type.*

4. *Identify at least three characteristics of the way people acquire their values.*

5. *List at least three features of a learning environment which promote values development.*

6. *Identify values and value indicators in your own life.*

All of the information needed to meet these objectives is presented in MEDIAPAK 1, in Part Two of the text *Values and Teaching,* and in this chapter, where the process of valuing is reviewed and expanded.

VALUING

Out of our life experiences we each acquire and develop values which guide our behavior. Values are the traces we leave behind as we go

through this life. Our values are implied in the communication and contacts we have with others, the causes we support, the memories we hold dear, the actions we take, and the ends to which we turn our life force.

Valuing, in our view, is defined by three processes—*choosing, prizing,* and *acting,* and for something to be called a value it must be:

1. Chosen freely,
2. Prized dearly,
3. Affirmed publicly,
4. Acted upon,
5. Part of a life pattern.

Valuing is a process which begins very early in our lives and continues throughout. Our values evolve and change just as our life experiences. Significant events in our lives—perhaps meeting a special person, getting a job, becoming a parent—may cause us to acquire new values or to modify established ones. Values may also vary with the setting in which we are interacting. There is likely no single value orientation which can enable every individual—or even one person—to function effectively in *all* life settings. Just as the ways we experience life, and the meaning we attach to our encounters with the world, are unique to us as individuals, so are values highly personalized. Being aware of our values and recognizing the validity of values which differ from our own lets us be more purposeful, more vital, and more integrated persons. Now let's look more closely at the five value criteria which were mentioned in MEDIAPAK 1.

1. Choosing. We have said that the first requirement for a value is that it be chosen *freely.* When there are meaningful options or alternatives open to us, then we can freely make choices or decisions. Such freedom of choice is essential to values development, for values are not acquired through coercion or force. Choice allows us to be a participant in, rather than an observer of, life. Values penetrate life itself; they are the result of personal choices we make willingly and of decisions we make after careful consideration of all the alternatives and their probable outcomes. Valuing, therefore, involves critical thinking, decision making, and problem solving.

2. Prizing. When we have chosen something ourselves, or for ourselves, it's likely to be very precious to us. Prizing is the second characteristic of a value, for valuing involves not only cognitive processes but the affective domain as well. Our feelings are important determiners of our values.

3. Affirming. Speaking out on an issue or a belief involves revealing quite a bit about yourself, and therefore a certain risk. People who are clear about their values, who know who they are and what they believe, are not afraid to say so. A value is something you are willing to affirm publicly and talk about to others.

4. Acting. Speaking or talking about what is of value in your life is not sufficient. If something is to meet our criteria for a value, it must be revealed in action. What we choose and cherish can only be fully realized

or experienced when we act upon it. Story writing, organic gardening, or becoming a nuclear physicist are not values in a person's life until that person writes some stories, plants and harvests a crop, or studies the required science courses.

5. Repeating.   Values form patterns in our lives; therefore, *repeating* is the final characteristic of a value. If a person writes *one* short story or poem, and never again sets pen to paper, we would not say that creative writing is a value for that person. The actions we take consistently and repeatedly reveal our values.

Value Indicators

While viewing MEDIAPAK 1, you were encouraged to examine what has value in *your* life. You were also asked to examine that "value" in terms of the five criteria we discussed. Some of you found that you had actually been thinking about a *value indicator*—an attitude, aspiration, activity, belief, feeling, goal, interest, purpose, or problem. Value indicators are also significant determiners of our behavior; in addition, they have an important relationship to the valuing process, for they have the potential for becoming actual values. For a more complete discussion of the categories of behavior which we call *value indicators,* you should refer to the text *Values and Teaching,* and later to MEDIAPAK 4.

TEACHING FOR VALUES DEVELOPMENT

Give a boy a fish and you feed him for a day. Teach him how to fish, and you feed him for life. (Chinese proverb, source unknown)

The process of valuing which we discussed can be taught through an approach called *Values Clarification.* Values clarification involves both thinking and feeling; its goal is to help individuals develop clear values by examining their own life experience. Each of the three processes involved in valuing—*choosing, prizing, acting*—can be accomplished, to a certain level, even by young children. There are growth periods, however, within each of the three processes, and what constitutes valuing at age seven is much less complex than valuing at age seventeen. The emphasis of the values clarification approach is on increasing the child's clarity of thinking, and therefore basis for thoughtful choosing, as he or she develops. Valuing is seen, in part, as a cognitive outcome of learning; competence in using the process of valuing increases developmentally as the child becomes able to think abstractly and to generalize. Once a strategy is learned, it becomes part of the person's cognitive structure and may then be used within, and often beyond, the problem situation in which it was taught (Ausubel and Robinson, 1969). Consequently, the *process* through which children acquire values is more important, we feel, than the actual values themselves. In other words, teaching the process of valuing, rather than specific values, provides children with a life-long strategy which can be used in broad categories of behavior. Valuing is not solely related to the cognitive aspects of human personality, however. Rather, it is a pervasive process which involves the whole personality— *affective* as well as cognitive aspects. Prizing and cherishing are deeply rooted in feelings; the meaning of what is prized or cherished is deeply personal and known only to the learner. For this reason, self-evaluation of experience and of value outcomes is central to values education. Only the learner can determine what is relevant, what is of value.

Values, we have said, derive from and evolve out of life experiences. Conversely, our values are important determiners of our perceptions and behavior. Hamachek explains this point clearly:

> We more readily perceive those things, experiences, and people we value, prize and esteem. For example, have you ever noticed your ability to spot the person you care for in a crowd of people, or your ability to see *your* name on an entire page of names? (1971, p. 37).

Teaching for values development, then, must be directed to the intellectual *and* feeling levels of individual learners. Values clarification is a powerful method of teaching for values development since it combines both cognitive and affective education and provides a structure for self-inquiry. Certain conditions must, however, be present in the learning environment for values development to take place. These conditions are briefly mentioned below and will be elaborated more fully in subsequent modules of this program.

An Environment for Values Development

The optimal environment for values development is one which is strongly interactive and supportive—an atmosphere in which *learning* takes precedence over *teaching*—and where meaningful, relevant learning is prized. Your ability to create such an environment in your classroom depends upon your capacity for respecting, discovering, and helping to maximize the uniqueness of each individual student. Students can learn and apply the process of valuing only in an environment where:

1. There is a deep respect for each student's personal experience.

2. A structure is provided for the examination and evaluation of experiences.

3. Freedom to choose among meaningful behavioral alternatives is allowed and encouraged.

4. Critical thinking and thoughtful decision making are made possible through teacher assistance.

5. Students' choices are respected by the teacher.

As teachers, we need to examine our own values as they relate to the lives of the children with whom we interact and then analyze how our values are translated into classroom practice. Schools have for centuries emphasized the importance of cognitive learning, and educators have long asserted that the function of the schools is to teach the learner to be intellectually competent. Recently this hard-headed approach has been challenged, and a number of approaches to expanding human consciousness and realizing individual potential are emerging. Values clarification is one such approach. If we as teachers are going to use it effectively, we must focus not solely on the facts, the books, the audiovisual information sources which fill our classrooms, but also on the relevance, meaning, and purpose the classroom has for the children who live in it. As Arthur Coombs writes in his article, "What Can Man Become?":

> We need to change the situation we sometimes find in our teaching where the impression is given the student that all the answers worth having lie "out there." I believe it is necessary for us to recognize that the only important answers are those which the individual has within himself, for these are the only ones that will ever show up in his behavior (1969, p. 17).

When you have completed this section, turn to the next page and do the *Self-Checking Exercise* for review.

Following the exercise you will find some Activities designed to assist you in applying some elements of the valuing process.

SELF-CHECKING EXERCISE

Note: More than one answer may be correct.

1. According to Raths' theory, values are considered to be:
   a) Universal moral principles.
   b) Ethical codes of society.
   c) Individual behavioral guides.
   d) Religious doctrines.

2. The most significant determiner of behavioral guides is our:
   a) Life experience.
   b) Intellectual ability.
   c) Emotions.
   d) Use of time.

3. How a person, through experience, obtains his or her values is more important than what values he or she holds, since:
   a) People in a given society hold the same values anyway.
   b) Individuals can have different values and still relate effectively to their environments.
   c) Experiential background differs from person to person.
   d) There is no question as to what values should be taught.

4. Though experiences, and therefore values, differ from person to person, each value must meet five requirements. The five criteria which define a value are:
   a)
   b)
   c)
   d)
   e)

5. Valuing is based on choosing, prizing, acting. Values, therefore, are the result of:
   a) Choosing freely from among alternatives.
   b) Trial-and-error learning.
   c) Practicing what we preach.
   d) Directed teaching.
   e) Repeated behaviors.

6. Not everything in our lives is a value. Personal expressions which have a significant relationship to valuing but which are not yet values are:

   a) Goals, purposes, aspirations.
   b) Value indicators.
   c) Attitudes, beliefs, convictions.
   d) Interests, feelings, worries.

7.   Value indicators include goals, purposes, aspirations, attitudes, beliefs, and convictions, as well as interests, feelings, and worries. In the list below, find the statements which include value indicators:
   a) I have been wanting to take up poetry.
   b) We hope to go to Europe next summer.
   c) I believe in men's lib.
   d) I worry about everything.
   e) I'm convinced there are too many people on welfare.

8.   Values are personal, enabling each of us to relate effectively and in our own best way to our surroundings. In addition, our values are likely to be:
   a) Firmly established in young adulthood.
   b) The result of a life-long process.
   c) Modified by significant life events.
   d) Evolving and maturing from day to day.
   e) Whatever seems right at the time.

9.   Discovering, developing, and refining our values means integrating our experiences into a meaningful pattern. Helping children with the valuing process requires:
   a)
   b)

10.   Teachers who respect a child's experience and who are willing to help that child examine that experience for values are involved in:
   a) Values clarification.
   b) Teaching right from wrong.
   c) Teaching for values development.
   d) Setting good examples.

11.   Some prerequisites for values clarification, or teaching for values development, are:
   a) Creating an environment of respect and trust.
   b) Being skilled in persuasion techniques.
   c) Presenting alternatives and allowing choice.
   d) Having control over the class.

12.   When teachers create a safe environment in which students can make choices and determine their own values, the students are likely to become _____.

If you want to help children achieve more and be more positive and enthusiastic in their approaches to life, do the following Activities to begin practicing some of the elements of values theory.

Activity 1

This activity may be completed individually, or with two or more persons working in pairs.

1.   List the initials of all the persons who come to your home to share a meal with you or to visit. Next, list the initials of all the persons you visit, drive to work or church, etc.

2.   Look at both of your lists. Note how many persons on your lists are relatives, and how many are friends or acquaintances. Calculate the percentage of relatives, of friends, of acquaintances.

3.   Look at your lists again and ask yourself these questions:
How many are black? How many are white?
How many are older? How many are younger than myself?
How many am I really happy to be with?
How many do I see often?
How many would I like to see more often?

4.   Finally, ask yourself, "Is there anything I want to change?" "What can I do about it?" "Will I do something about it?" Discuss.

Activity 2

1. Begin to keep a log of your own personal value indicators—a list of your hopes, dreams, beliefs, and so on.

2. Periodically look at your log. Ask yourself, "Will I do anything about this goal (attitude, fear. . .)?" "Have I done anything about this?"

3. As time passes, note which of your value indicators actually become values in your life.

2

Values: Saying Who You Are

Before beginning to read this chapter, view the MEDIAPAK audio-visual component labeled "2, Values: Saying Who You Are."

When you have completed both the media and print portions of this module, you will be able to:

1. *Explain how values clarification differs from traditional methods of values education.*

2. *List teacher characteristics which are critical in helping students develop values.*

3. *List seven ways in which teacher-facilitators interact with students.*

4. *Assess your own readiness for being a facilitator of values development.*

5. *Identify changes you will make in your classroom environment and in your interaction with students.*

All of the information needed to meet these objectives is presented in MEDIAPAK 2, in Parts Two and Four of the text *Values and Teaching*, and in this chapter, where teaching for value clarity is discussed.

THE ESSENCE OF VALUING

Valuing is a process which results from our interactions with people, ideas, and events. Our approach to values development is based on the belief that each individual is unique and that each person has the potential for being everything that he or she is. Becoming, or developing and extending your potential as a person, depends upon discovering, understanding, and enjoying your own uniqueness. It involves thinking *and* feeling, being *and* acting. We express or show who we are—how we think, feel, live—by our values. Valuing is not a matter of complying with rules or principles we've been taught, nor of modeling our behavior patterns on those of others, for this kind of learning involves only the mind. Rather, valuing is a matter of exploring, accepting, enhancing, and changing ourselves as individuals, of engaging in the kind of learning which involves our hearts and our souls, as well as our minds.

VALUING IN THE CLASSROOM

Our approach to helping children develop values, which we call *values clarification*, does not depend on direct instruction or on imparting or attempting to instill certain values in the minds of our students. Values clarification does not use appeals to conscience, nor does it rely on cultural or religious dogma. Indoctrination violates the requirement that a value must be freely chosen. In contrast to the traditional methods of teaching values or providing moral education, values clarification is based on the efficacy, or power, of what Rogers calls "experiential learning" (1969, p. 5). Rogers defines this kind of learning as learning which:

1. Has a *quality of personal involvement,*
2. Is *self-initiated,*
3. Is *pervasive* —making a "difference in the behavior, the attitudes, perhaps even in the personality of the learner,"
4. *Is evaluated by the learner,*
5. Is *meaningful* to the learner.

It is through *this* kind of learning that values—values that are chosen, prized, acted upon—develop.

In the MEDIAPAK accompanying this section, we acknowledge that not everyone will readily agree on, or decide to utilize, our approach to values development. We pointed out that some people feel that children are too inexperienced in life to be trusted to make appropriate decisions. Others feel that children should be able to rely on adults to tell them what

to believe, and how to act, and that without firm direction children will be insecure. Such arguments are not totally invalid; however, they miss the essential point that we are making: *acquiring clear and meaningful values requires practice*. Without the opportunity to personally experience and use the process of valuing, children cannot be expected to develop values which are their own and which will increase their senses of self-worth and identity, enabling them to reach new and higher levels of fulfillment. Naturally we are not suggesting that children can decide everything for themselves, or that adults should not provide guidelines. We are saying, instead, that even young children can benefit from the chance to make some choices, however limited, about what is important in their lives, and that children who are given this chance are more likely to grow up to be persons who know the joy of realizing who they really are.

If this view of children is compatible with your own, and if you are willing to act upon it openly with your students, *you* can facilitate values development.

Being a Facilitator

Being a *facilitator* puts the emphasis on learning rather than on teaching. Being a facilitator demands commitment, flexibility, involvement, and patience. Romey describes it as:

> A relationship in which the facilitator is constantly available to the learners who are working with him, is vitally interested in them as people, and is constantly concerned about providing an opportunity for them to develop emotionally, physically, and intellectually (1972, p. 115).

As a facilitator, you cannot hide behind facts and information; you must be who *you* are, know your own feelings, and be able to live with them. You must project yourself as a *real* person, not as a role. That is what it means to bring *yourself* into the learning situation.

In MEDIAPAK 2, we mentioned seven ways of interacting with students, or seven things a teacher-facilitator can do to help students clarify their values:

1. Encourage students to make choices and allow them to choose freely.

2. Help them to examine available alternatives.

3. Suggest that students weigh each alternative carefully and reflect on its possible consequences before making a choice.

4. Encourage students to look within—to consider what it is they prize and cherish.

5. Give students the opportunity to affirm their choices publicly.

6. Encourage students to act and live in accordance with their choices.

7. Help students examine repeated behaviors, or patterns, in their lives.

Each of these seven ways of relating to students and of facilitating values clarification requires that the teacher create an open, supportive learning environment, a place where there is *freedom* to learn, *trust* in each student's capacity for growth, and finally, *respect* for each student as a unique individual. Now, let's look more closely at each of these important and very interdependent teacher behaviors.

1. Trust.   A learning environment which has the kind of openness and freedom we have described must be built on trust and used to promote trust. "This trust is something which cannot be faked. It is not a technique" (Rogers, 1969, p. 75). The teacher-facilitator must deeply believe in people and trust in their capacity to develop their potential, their humanness—both as individuals and as a group. It is only because you don't trust in people that you feel you have to *tell* them what to do to prevent them from going their own "misguided" way. When trust is there, students will be able and willing to risk expressing their true feelings and thoughts, for they will know that the teacher will accept them as they are and support their need to be and become who they are. Acceptance is a critical aspect of trust. Trust permits us to give freedom and allow choice.

2. Freedom.   The best environment for experiential learning is one in which students feel accepted, supported, and free to be themselves—a climate where it is safe to express one's thoughts and feelings. There is a place for everyone, an atmosphere of openness and sharing.

To create such an environment, the teacher must be open to the varied suggestions and ideas that students have, and willing to allow them as much freedom to choose what they want to learn and what they want to do as possible. Choice, freedom, and self-direction are basic to values development and values clarification. The kind of freedom we are describing does not mean total permissiveness, and so it does not lead to chaos and confusion. Our notion of freedom and openness in the learning environment is based on the premise that "in general the enlargement of people's freedom tends to promote their interest because it provides more opportunities for the discovery of what is good" (Peters, 1967, p. 116). "What is good" is that which, out of all the possibilities allowable in a classroom, meets the needs of individual learners.

The limits beyond which students' choices are restricted must be clearly defined if both the teacher and the students are going to be able to function effectively in the learning environment. As Rogers says:

the *amount* of freedom which can be given to a group is not particularily important . . . what is important is that within those limits the freedom that is given is *real*, is not hesitantly or guardedly given by the leader, and it is perceived as real by the students (1969, p. 74).

3. Respect.   Being a facilitator for values clarification means being a person who respects and prizes the learner, however imperfect he or she may be, as one who is full of potential. There is great power, almost magic, about the kind of student-teacher relationship where the student feels understood, not judged or evaluated, but simply *understood* by the teacher. If a student risks self-disclosure—takes a stand; makes a choice—he or she is vulnerable. If the teacher does not respond and react in a manner which conveys respect for the student's point of view, that student will be unlikely to risk again in the presence of that teacher. *Trust, freedom,* and *respect* are "givens" for values clarification.

When you have completed this section, turn to the next page and do the Activities. These Activities are designed to be done independently.

Activity 3

Throughout this chapter, and in MEDIAPAK 2, we emphasized that there are certain attitudes and teacher behaviors which are critical to the effective classroom use of values clarification methods. The following activity is presented to help you *review* what we consider to be the major teacher characteristics and preliminary steps toward becoming a facilitator of the valuing process with your students. Notice that this activity is actually a personal rating scale to enable you to *assess your own potential* as a values teacher. An opportunity will be provided at the end of this program for you to complete the questionnaire a second time so that you may determine the ways in which you've grown and changed. Respond to the items as candidly as you are able; you *will not* be asked to share your responses with anyone else—though you may certainly do so if you wish.

Rating Scale for Teacher-Facilitators of Values Education

Directions: Write today's date here _____ and rank yourself, as of *this* point in time, on all of the following variables:

	1 hardly ever	2 sometimes	3 often	4 almost always
1. I act as though I believe students are capable of self-directed learning.				
2. When I meet students for the first time, I look for the uniqueness in each one.				
3. I seek ways to enhance both cognitive *and* affective development in students.				
4. I take responsibility for trying to help meet some of the emotional needs of students I work with.				
5. I grow and learn through my interactions with the people around me.				
6. I try to get to know students as persons.				

	1 hardly ever	2 sometimes	3 often	4 almost always
7. I take time to examine *my* personal feelings, attitudes, values.				
8. I am clear about certain values of my own.				
9. I am working on clarifying some of my own values.				
10. I attempt to guide rather than direct student learning, and I let students think for themselves.				
11. I make alternative tasks, activities, responses available to students.				
12. I encourage students to suggest their own alternatives.				
13. I allow freedom of choice among the available alternatives.				
14. I encourage and assist students to weigh their choices and to consider possible consequences of their actions both in and outside the classroom.				
15. I ask students questions about what is important to them, what they prize in life.				
16. I encourage students to examine their beliefs, attitudes, feelings for meaning.				
17. I allow students to verbally express their opinions, convictions, and values and support them in doing so.				
18. I try to listen and hear what students are saying in their words and actions.				
19. I define the classroom structure and limits I feel to be essential.				
20. I respect the lives and rights of students.				

If most of your responses are 4's or 3's, you are already prepared to begin learning and trying some values clarification strategies with students. While there are other characteristics which could have been included, all twenty attributes describe behaviors which (in our opinion) are essential to facilitating the process of valuing. If you are seriously interested in using values clarification with your students, you should be striving to attain these twenty characteristics. The following list of resources is intended to guide you in your personal quest.

Resources for Teacher-Facilitators

1. Johnson, D. W. *Reaching Out: Interpersonal Effectiveness and Self-Actualization*. Englewood Cliffs, N.J.: Prentice-Hall, 1972.
2. Rogers, C. R. *Freedom to Learn*. Columbus, Ohio: Charles E. Merrill, 1969.
3. Romey, W. D. *Risk—Trust—Love: Learning in a Humane Environment*. Columbus, Ohio: Charles E. Merrill, 1972.
4. Silberman, M. L., Allender, J. S., and Yanoff, J. M. *Real Learning: A Sourcebook for Teachers*. Boston: Little, Brown, 1976.
5. Volkmor, C. B., Langstaff, A. L., and Higgins, M. *Structuring the Classroom for Success*. Columbus, Ohio: Charles E. Merrill, 1974.

Activity 4

1. In the space below, list three things you would like to do in your classroom to create an environment which is more facilitative of values development:

a)

b)

c)

2. Put a circle around the one you want to work on first. List some ways you will go about making this change in your classroom environment or in your behavior.
My Action List:

3. Try out the things you listed above. At the end of each week make a statement about the results. Continue to act on your second and third choices in the same manner.

Activity 5

As you work through the modules in this program on *Values in the Classroom*, you will likely have some questions and concerns about values clarification in the classroom. Perhaps you have some already. Use the space below to write down your questions and concerns. Add to this list as you continue with the program.

WHERE DOES IT ALL LEAD?

If *trust, freedom*, and *respect* say something about you as a person and as a teacher, then you will likely be very interested in the next three modules, which are designed to show you how to use specific methods for values clarification in your classroom. The preceding exercises and activities perhaps gave you a chance to assess your potential for using such methods effectively and for having a facilitative relationship with your students. Maybe you learned something more, or even something new, about yourself. Awareness and knowledge about yourself for the purpose of fully experiencing the joy of your own humanity is what values clarification is all about. Alan Watts says it well:

> Just as true humor is laughter at oneself, true humanity is knowledge of oneself. Other creatures may love and laugh, talk and think, but it seems to be the special peculiarity of human beings that they reflect: they think about thinking and know that they know. This, like other feedback systems, may lead to vicious circles and confusions if improperly managed, but self-awareness makes humans resonant. It imparts that simultaneous "echo" to all that we think and feel as the box of a violin reverberates with the sound of the strings. It gives depth and volume to what would otherwise be shallow and flat (1966, p. 129).

Before viewing MEDIAPAK 3, read the preface to modules 3, 4, and 5.

Values Clarification
Methods: A Preface

In module 1, we presented our theory of values, including the five criteria for a value. In module 2, we talked about teacher characteristics which are critical in helping students develop their own values. You have had the opportunity to assess your own readiness for being a facilitator of values development. With this introduction and background in the values theory and rationale in mind, we now move into some specific methods for values clarification. It is time to translate the theory into practical applications for the classroom. In the next three modules (modules 3, 4, and 5), a variety of methods will be presented. First, in module 3, we will discuss "Written Activities," some designed for use with groups of students and some more appropriately used with individuals. Next, in module 4, "The Clarifying Response" will be presented. The Clarifying Response is a technique for use with individuals only. Finally, in module 5, we will focus on various "Discussion Activities."

PRESENTATION
SEQUENCE

We have chosen this particular sequence ("Written Activities," "The Clarifying Response," and "Discussion Activities") because we feel there is a difference among the methods in level of difficulty. The last two methods take more skill and practice to implement successfully.

It is our opinion that written activities may be the easiest to develop and use, especially when you are just getting into using values clarification. Written methods are also least threatening to both teachers and students. Using the Clarifying Response usually demands a change in your thinking and a new way of responding to what students say. You will need some additional familiarity with the valuing process and increased skill and practice if you want to be successful with the Clarifying Response technique. Values discussions are mostly group activities and must be handled carefully and skillfully. Discussion involves the greatest degree of public disclosure of attitudes, feelings, and beliefs and the greatest risk taking by the participants.

In summary, we suggest that you begin with some of the written methods and work up to those that involve discussion.

A WORD ABOUT
CURRICULUM AND VALUES

Integrating values with curriculum means giving personal meaning to the content a student is studying. *All* the methods presented here can be integrated and used in just about any course—even P.E. and Typing. Whenever an issue becomes apparent; whenever there is a place for a comparison of other cultures, ideas, or feelings; whenever there is a theme, moral, or purpose—the topic may be ripe for a values exercise. Help students relate the topic or issue personally to their own lives. Help students learn to consider the value implications of whatever they are studying and learning. In module 3, we show specifically how values and curriculum can be integrated, but as you are going through the rest of the methods, try to think of how each one can be related to one or more of the curricular areas. Any of our sample Values Sheets, for example, could also be material for a values discussion.

Now, let's get on with values clarification methods, and begin with "Written Activities."

3

Values Clarification
Methods: Written
Activities

Before beginning to read this chapter, view the MEDIAPAK audio-visual components labeled "3, Values Clarification Methods: Written Activities."

When you have completed both the media and print portions of this module, you will be able to:

1. *Identify six written methods for values clarification.*

2. *Identify the two major components of the Values Sheet.*

3. *Develop a values sheet in the style of the valuing theory.*

4. *List five additional methods for written values clarification activities.*

5. *Implement at least one of the remaining five written methods.*

All of the information needed to meet these objectives is presented in MEDIAPAK 3, in Part Three of the text *Values and Teaching* and in this chapter, where the written values clarification methods are reviewed and expanded.

This chapter focuses on written activities which can be developed and presented to groups of students or individuals. These written methods are the Values Sheet, the Thought Sheet, Weekly Reaction Sheets, Open-Ended Questions, Coding Student Papers, and Time Diary.

THE VALUES SHEET

In the MEDIAPAK we showed how the Values Sheet consists of two major parts: a provocative statement designed to bring a general interest issue to the students' attention and a series of questions related to that statement. The questions are designed in the style of the valuing theory and carry the student through the criteria of choosing, prizing, and acting. Students respond to a Values Sheet on their own, with their own thoughts and feelings.

Some Tips on Developing Values Sheets

Some general suggestions to keep in mind when developing and using Values Sheets are:

1. Avoid loading the dice in favor of or against an issue.

5. Every sheet should contain a choice to be made, with alternatives to consider, and should point to consequences.

Implementation

1. Pass the sheet out to students with no discussion except perhaps to read over the statement and questions.

2. Allow enough time for all who participate to reflect on the questions and respond to them on their own. Values Sheets are ideal for take-home activities, to allow students enough time to think about the issue *on their own.*

3. After a suitable length of time for writing, a discussion might ensue. A discussion need not always follow a Values Sheet; but if it does, it should be general and brief.

2. Aim for expression of the fullest range of opinions.

3. Allow students time to think, reflect, and respond independently.

The Topic

Here are some points to keep in mind when selecting and developing the topic for a Values Sheet.

1. Make sure the topic appeals to your students; listen to them and follow the leads they reveal in their everyday conversations and activities.

2. Focus in on the central issue as clearly as possible. Eliminate anything that is extraneous or not to the point.

3. Have general objectives in mind as to what you want your students to gain.

4. Decide on the format. Is the topic you've chosen best handled as a Values Sheet? Or is it better handled via another written method or a discussion activity?

5. Make the topic relevant to what students are studying currently.

The Questions

1. Select the step or steps of the valuing process you are going to include as questions (choosing, prizing, acting). It is probably best to begin with one step at first (for example, develop several questions related to choosing and examining alternatives, instead of trying to hit all the steps at once).

2. "You" questions are basic to Values Sheets and encourage the student to relate the topic or issue to himself.

3. Avoid "why" questions.

4. Limit the number of questions to two or three, especially when the technique is new to you or when you are using it with younger children.

SELF-CHECKING EXERCISE

The following steps are designed to help you review the critical features of the *Values Sheet* and construct one for your students.*

1. A *Values Sheet* is a structured writing activity for use with groups of students. The Values Sheet consists of two parts. These are:
   a)
   b)

2. The provocative statement on the Values Sheet can be drawn from topics of general interest. List *three* topics which might be of interest to your students:
   a)
   b)
   c)

3. Remember that material for Values Sheets can be drawn from many sources: field trips, political events, textbooks, the media. Now, select *one* of the topics you listed in question **2** above and list the source(s) from which you could draw your material.

4. Gather or obtain any material(s) needed for your Values Sheet.

5. The statement at the top of a Values Sheet can be one or several short paragraphs, one sentence, or a reading assignment. Now, on page 43, write the statement which forms the basis of your Values Sheet. Include directions or instructions to the student where necessary.

6. Reread the statement you have written and ask yourself if it will really stimulate independent thinking and decision making on the part of your students. Modify the statement if necessary.

*If you are not working with students at this time, you may design a Values Sheet for a colleague to try out.

7. The second part of the Values Sheet is a short series of questions. The questions are designed around the crucial processes of valuing theory, which are:
    a)
    b)
    c)

8. Keep the criteria of choosing, prizing, and acting in mind as you frame your questions. Avoid revealing your own point of view by the way you phrase the questions.

9. Now, return to your Values Sheet and write the questions you wish students to consider.

10. Reread your questions to see if they probe the valuing process (choosing, prizing, acting). Revise if necessary.

11. When you have completed your Values Sheet, take a look at the samples provided on the following pages.

12. Critique your Values Sheet by using the checklist on page 47.

13. If your Values Sheet meets all of the criteria listed on the checklist, you may wish to duplicate it and try it out on a few students later.

Values Sheet I

Following the instructions listed on pages 41 and 42, design your Values Sheet in the space below.

SAMPLE
VALUES SHEETS

On the following pages, we present a few examples of Values Sheets and formats. For more examples, refer to the text *Values and Teaching*.

Example A. (These two examples, based on the theme of "economic choice," illustrate the use of questions alone.)

---

1. Write down the name of something you want that you don't have. List all the ways you might get it. How long would it take? Who might help? What can you do about it?

---

2. When you have 50¢ to spend, what kinds of choices must you make? How do your choices depend on your values?

Example B. Here is an example illustrating the use of pictures, prints, cartoons, etc., as the stimulus.

Select a picture which depicts a holiday celebration—for example, Thanksgiving.

Picture of Thanksgiving Celebration

1. What is a ritual?
2. How important are rituals in people's lives?
3. How important are holidays to you?
4. What makes this holiday special to you?
5. What would you change or not change about the way you celebrate Thanksgiving?

Example C.   This Values Sheet is shown in MEDIAPAK 3, related to the study of the Bill of Rights. It illustrates using an excerpt from a speech, a book, or document as the topic.

The Bill of Rights—First Amendment

Congress shall make no law restricting an establishment of religion, or prohibiting the free exercise thereof; or abridging the freedom of speech, or of the press; or the right of the people peaceably to assemble and to petition the government for a redress of grievances.

1. What rights are protected in the First Amendment?
2. What does "freedom of the press" mean?
3. What would happen if newspapers were told what they could or could not print?
4. What does the freedom guaranteed by the First Amendment mean to you?

Example D.   This Values Sheet relates to the study of the westward movement and women's role in society. This example and Example E illustrate the use of a single statement or quotation as the basis from which the questions are drawn.

"A woman needs only the education necessary for work in the home."

  1. What economic roles did women play in the frontier days?

  2. Which of these roles do women play in America today?

  3. How are the roles of women today different?

  4. How do you feel about the roles of women in today's society?

Example E. This is a Values Sheet related to consumer education.

"A Penny Saved Is a Penny Earned." . . . or "Buy Now—Pay Later"

  1. Is installment buying a way to save money?

  2. Why do people buy on credit when it costs more?

  3. What kinds of things do you think people should save for?

  4. What kinds of things do you think people should buy on credit?

Example F. A Values Sheet can be based on a common reading, in this case a chapter in a social studies book.

  1. What are some things the Hopi Indians value?
  2. What are some things you value in your life?
  3. How have our values changed?

CHECKLIST FOR
EFFECTIVE VALUE SHEETS

                                                                    Yes | No

1. The topic is of general interest.

2. The statement is at an appropriate reading level for the students.

3. The list of questions is short (3 or 4).

4. "Yes–No," "either–or," "why" questions are not included.

5. The questions avoid revealing the teacher's point of view or implying "right" answers. (Don't you think it is wise to . . .?)

6. The questions are built around *choosing, prizing, acting* —getting children to make choices, state reasons, list possible consequences.

7. Many of the questions are "you" questions— which is the essence.

8. There is at least one question related to actual behavior—what the student does or intends to do.

When you have completed this section, turn to the next page and do the Activities. These Activities are designed to provide the opportunity to practice and experience the methods before implementing them with students.

Activity 6

This is an Activity to be done on your own.

1. Select a quote or item from your local newspaper which documents a values-related public event or story.

2. Respond to the following questions as related to your newsclipping:

What do you agree with?

What do you disagree with?

3. Now, try to rewrite the quote or statement so it reflects your *own* opinion.

Activity 7

This activity is also designed to be completed independently.

　　1. Select one of the following quotations (or one of your own), and develop two or three questions that get at the meaning of the quotation and relate it to your life.

> Grant that I may not criticize my neighbor until I have walked a mile in his moccasins.　　(an Indian prayer)

> I have been to the mountaintop . . . . I had a dream. (Martin Luther King)

> Man ceases to be free the moment he makes freedom a goal. . . .　　(Kahlil Gibran)

> Some men see things as they are and say "why?" I dreamed of things that never were and said, "why not?"　　(Robert Kennedy)

> One's man justice is another's injustice; one man's beauty, another's ugliness; one man's wisdom, another's folly.　　(Ralph Waldo Emerson)

Quote:

Questions:

Activity 8

This activity is designed for use with small groups. You will need at least two small groups with 2 to 4 persons in each.

1. Begin reading the daily newspaper for articles dealing with values-related topics in your own community and state and the rest of the world. Each group clips out an article.

2. Break into small groups (in a college classroom or workshop setting). Each group takes a clipping and discusses the issue.

3. As a group, formulate a statement based on the issue in the clipping. Write your statement here:

4. Now, develop two or three questions based on the statement and the valuing criteria of choosing, prizing, and acting. Write your questions here:

5. Exchange your Values Sheet with another small group. Each group member should read the statement on your new Values Sheet and respond to the questions on a separate piece of paper. Remember, think about the questions on your own and write independently.

6. Discuss this activity either in your small group or with the total group, if you wish.

OTHER
WRITTEN METHODS

In the second half of MEDIAPAK 3, we gave a brief overview of some written methods which are less structured than the Values Sheet. These additional methods are reviewed and examples provided for each on the following pages. All of these methods are covered in even more detail in *Values and Teaching.*

Thought Sheets

Thought Sheets are little cards or papers used by students to record any value-related idea or thought that has occupied their attention during the week. One card should be filled out per week. This method is best used in a regular pattern with students. The ideas are student generated, not initiated by the teacher. Thought Sheets are usually brief, often only a few words—one thought. Students turn their Thought Sheets in at the end of the week, and the teacher may respond with a note or a brief conference. Thought Sheets may be saved and returned to their originator after a few weeks or midway through the term. At that time, the students can be asked to summarize and analyze them. One tip: before initiating this activity, it is helpful to have a class discussion on what the word "value" means. Also, see *Values and Teaching* for an example of how to introduce Thought Sheets to a class. Here are some examples of some Thought Sheets written by third-grade students early in the school year.

> This week I played tennis and my tennis teacher said I played good because I didn't play good before. It made me feel good.

> This week I was happy when I won a contest. I had to ride Sky Rocket, my horse on a very hard obstical course.

> I went to my Den Meeting and I earned some beads.

> We went down to the lizard place and caught fifteen baby frogs and my friend gave me a lizard.

> We are moving to a new house.

Try keeping your own Thought Sheets for several weeks.

Weekly Reaction Sheets

Weekly Reaction Sheets, like Thought Sheets, are best used in a regular patterned way, weekly and over time. Students respond to a few questions designed to help them examine the past week's activities—what they did and how they spent their time. Allow class time for students to sit down and ponder the past week or ask them to respond at home. Ask students to examine the presence or absence of activities they personally selected, to think about how the week could have been better or about what they learned that was valuable and could prove useful in their life.

When Weekly Reaction Sheets are collected, the teacher may make a brief written or verbal comment or question.

Here are some examples of some weekly reaction sheets written by third-grade students.

Question: "What did you do this week that made you proud?"

I made my first communion.

I got up on waterskis

I helped my sister when she was sick

Questions: Are you happy with the way you spend your weekends? How could you improve them?

I could think about my weekend ahead of time and plan things.

I could improve my weekend by cleaning my room

I am happy with my weekend because I go to church but I could improve it with a family home evening every Sunday.

I am happy with the way I spend my weekends. I don't have to change it because it was perfect.

Open-Ended Questions

Regrettably, "What I Did for Summer Vacation" is probably the only personal topic all year in many English Composition classes. Open-Ended Questions is an especially good technique for use with younger students. For very young children, responses can be dictated to and written by the teacher, as in the "Language Experience" approach to reading. Children love to share their feelings and beliefs. This technique can be used spontaneously and irregularly. Many examples of Open-Ended Questions are found in *Values and Teaching.* Here are two more which are a bit more complicated.

My ideal is . . .
How can you reach your ideal? What can you do? How is your ideal different from what exists now?

(This example illustrates how an Open-Ended Question can be combined with other values questions. Let the students respond to the question "My ideal is . . ." first. Then present the other questions to help students reflect on what they wrote.)

> If I had ten minutes in a department store and could choose any items I wanted free, I would choose. . . .

Here are some responses to Open-Ended Questions as dictated to their teacher by some young children.

My best friend always . . .
        buys me ice cream.
        lets me borrow something.
        shakes hands with me.
        sits by me.
        plays with me.
        goes bike riding.

If someone gave me $100 . . .
        I would give it to the President.
        I'd buy a motorcycle.
        I'd buy a bike.
        I'd give half back to the person who gave it to me.
        I'd buy a dog.
        I'd give it to poor people.
        I would buy a pool for the summer or I might put it in the bank and save it for college and the money would grow and I will have more money.

I feel happy when . . .
>I play.
>I do something important like fixing cars.
>my birthday comes.
>I get a Charlie Brown award at School.
>I am with my parents.
>I am with my friends.
>I go to school.
>I make a new friend.

I feel sad when . . .
>someone doesn't share.
>my friend fights.
>I don't go to school.
>nobody is talking to me.
>I have nothing to do.
>no one comes to my house.

What I like most . . .
>The thing I like most is taking care of my animals. Why? Because they are important to me and it's fun watching them grow up and look beautiful.
>What I like most is to have a party. What I like most is camping.
>I like to climb in a tree and nobody to bug me, that's what I like.

Coding Student Papers

Remember, this technique involves putting a + beside a statement in a written theme or paper that the student seems to be for and a − beside statements the student may be against or unclear about. With practice and a different orientation, you can do this very quickly while correcting a student's work. Do not do it on all students' written work, only on those papers where the topics are likely to elicit value-related expressions. To practice this technique, you might try it on yourself. Find a term paper or (even better) an old letter to or from a friend and read it over. Mark the values indicator statements with either a + or a −.

Time Diary

The Time Diary focuses sharply on how one uses his time. It can be kept by half-hour periods, by the hour, or by the day. Students can be asked to keep a diary for several weeks and then asked to review what they wrote and summarize what they learned about themselves from studying their diaries. Did any patterns emerge? Did you make any changes in how you spent your time?

You may wish to keep your own Time Diary.

This completes our chapter on "Written Activities." At this point you may wish to take a little break from this program and actually try implementing one or more of these methods with some students.

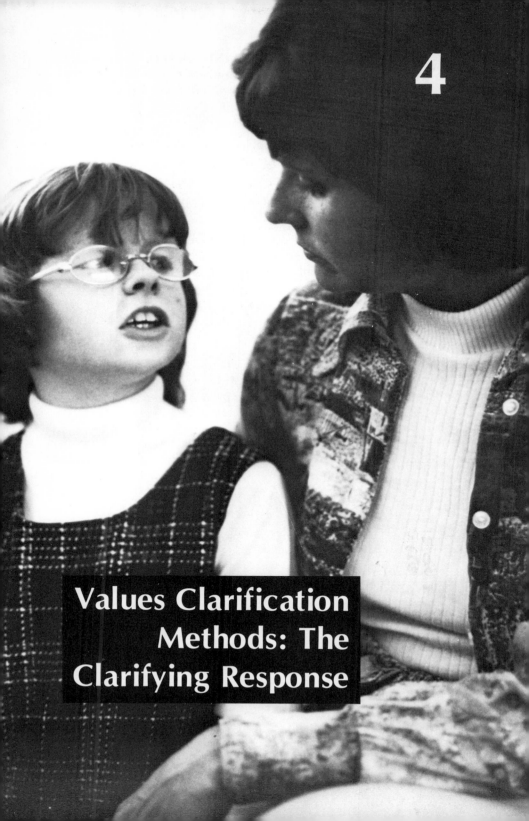

4

Values Clarification Methods: The Clarifying Response

Before beginning to read this chapter, view the MEDIAPAK audio-visual components labeled "4, Values Clarification Methods: The Clarifying Response."

When you have completed both the media and print portions of this module, you will be able to:

1. *Describe a Clarifying Response and how it is used.*

2. *Identify five categories of Value Indicator statements.*

3. *List some criteria of an effective Clarifying Response.*

4. *Formulate and verbalize Clarifying Responses related to the five categories of Value Indicators.*

All of the information needed to meet these objectives is presented in MEDIAPAK 4, in Part Three of the text *Values and Teaching,* and in this chapter, where the Clarifying Response and Value Indicators are reviewed and expanded.

THE CLARIFYING RESPONSE

The greatest effect of the question is the way and extent to which it causes the pupil to think (Cunningham, 1971).

In the MEDIAPAK, you saw how the Clarifying Response is used as a method for responding to student statements or actions. It is a carefully

formulated, open-ended question designed to encourage the student to think about his ideas or look at his behavior and decide for himself what he wants, what he can do, what he feels. In so doing, he takes steps toward clarifying his thinking. The Clarifying Response is a method of responding to what students say with a question, not an answer.

IDENTIFYING VALUE INDICATOR STATEMENTS

Clarifying Responses are most appropriately used in situations where students are expressing ideas, thoughts, and feelings related to their *attitudes,* their *aspirations,* their *purposes,* their *interests,* and their *activities.* Statements related to those categories have a personal meaning to the individual—and may reveal thoughts or behaviors that are on their way to becoming values.

Let's review briefly the five categories of statements called *Value Indicators.*

1. Attitudes—statements which reveal something a person is *for* or *against;*

2. Aspirations—statements which reveal a long-time goal or plan;

3. Purposes—statements which reveal a short-range goal or hope;

4. Interests—statements which reveal what an individual likes to do in his or her free time;

5. Activities—statements which reveal how an individual *uses* his time.

To effectively use the clarifying question or statement to respond to Value Indicator statements, the teacher will need a new orientation and some attention and practice.

FORMULATING A
CLARIFYING QUESTION

The Clarifying Question must stimulate thinking; most often questions that teachers ask do *not* stimulate critical thinking but instead are used to initiate instruction, correct misbehavior, or manage classroom behavior. When you stop to think about it, most of the questions we ask students in the classroom require short, factual answers. We use questions to collect

information, verify ideas, and review. Questions such as "What is the capital of Georgia?" or "How much are 2 + 2?" are examples of the *narrow* or convergent question used every day during instruction (Cunningham, 1971).

Challenging a student to think, weigh alternatives, and examine his values requires *broader* questions. Broad questions encourage a wide variety of responses, and are designed to be thought provoking and to motivate students to explore subjects more deeply. Questions such as "How do you feel about farming as an occupation?" or "What makes you wish to live in Australia?" ask a student to organize her thoughts, formulate an opinion, and select her own opinion or position. Divergent questions such as these open up a range of possibilities; they may lead a student to new insights and new appreciations, and help him clarify his thinking.

As teachers, we can learn through practice to use broad, open-ended questions more often in our everyday teaching. By simply changing the wording of the questions we ask, we can change the level of thought required by the question.

USING THE CLARIFYING RESPONSE

Here are some tips for using the Clarifying Response effectively.

1.   Begin slowly. Aim for one Clarifying Response per day at first until you "get the feel" of it.

2.   Be brief; use one question or comment. Clarifying responses take place in passing—at recess, before school, during lunch, or in class.

3.   Use selectively, only with one or two students at first and only those students who make a *personal* statement about a belief, an interest, or an aspiration.

4.   Avoid "why" questions or questions which may prod the students to justify or defend what they said.

5.   Do not deliver an answer. Learn to be comfortable with *silence* to allow personal thinking to happen. We often overlook the use of the "pause" as an effective tool in facilitating thinking. We are more often too anxious and ready to jump in with "the answer."

When you have completed this section, turn to the next page and do the *Self-Checking Exercise* for review. Following the Exercise, you will find some Activities designed to assist you in applying the Clarifying Response.

SELF-CHECKING EXERCISE

1. Throughout this module we focus on value-clarifying methods which require oral (as opposed to written) interactions with individual students. The Clarifying Response has which of the following features:

   a) Designed to teach new ideas.
   b) Is a method of responding to something a student says.
   c) Can be either a brief comment *or* a question.
   d) Gives the teacher the opportunity to interpret students' statements.
   e) Is intended to stimulate the student to look at his or her own ideas.

2. Answers b), c), and e) above describe the Clarifying Response. Check the questions in the list below which are examples of Clarifying Responses:

   a) How is this important to you?
   b) What other approaches have you considered?
   c) What does your father think about this?
   d) In what ways was the choice a happy one?
   e) Don't you think it would be best to _____?

3. Questions a), b), and d) are all examples of Clarifying Responses. Knowing when to use such responses is largely a matter of listening closely to what students are saying. Write some expressions below which are cues or Value Indicators.

   a) I feel so happy when . . .
   b)
   c)
   d)

4. Your expressions should include words such as *hope, like, want,* for such words reveal a person's aspirations, interests, attitudes, feelings, beliefs, goals, and purposes—all of which say something about values. Now, for each expression you wrote in question **3**, write a Clarifying Response.

   a) What helps to bring about those feelings?
   b)
   c)
   d)

5.   Clarifying Responses can be used informally by the teacher to help individual students test consequences, examine the reality of his or her choices, take the first step toward realizing a dream—or raise an activity to the value level. Therefore Clarifying Responses are:

    a) Critical commentaries.
    b) Positive and open-ended.
    c) Evaluations or judgments.
    d) Spontaneous.
    e) Permissive and stimulating.

6.   If you marked b), d), and e), you have learned the important features of the Clarifying Response. Now go on for more activities on their design and use.

Activity 9

Think up a question or several questions you would ask to help students clarify their thinking if you heard the following statements.

1. Attitude: I believe that the U.S. should not trade with Communist nations.

Which of the valuing criteria are your questions related to?
( ) Choosing.
( ) Prizing.
( ) Affirming.
( ) Acting.
( ) Repeating.

2. Aspiration: Someday, I am going to be a pediatrician.

Which of the valuing criteria are your questions related to?
( ) Choosing.
( ) Prizing.
( ) Affirming.
( ) Acting.
( ) Repeating.

3. Purpose: I'm thinking about applying for a job as a camp counselor this summer.

Which of the valuing criteria are your questions related to?

( ) Choosing.
( ) Prizing.
( ) Affirming.
( ) Acting.
( ) Repeating.

4. Interests: I really enjoy reading about electronics.

Which of the valuing criteria are your questions related to?

( ) Choosing.
( ) Prizing.
( ) Affirming.
( ) Acting.
( ) Repeating.

5. Activities: I spend my weekends working on my ham radio equipment.

Which of the valuing criteria are your questions related to?

( ) Choosing.
( ) Prizing.
( ) Affirming.
( ) Acting.
( ) Repeating.

Activity 10

1. With your family, at a party, or in a classroom with students, listen for statements that reveal attitudes, aspirations, purposes, interests, activities, or feelings.

2. Take one Value Indicator at a time—mentally formulate a possible Clarifying Response.

3. Later, try verbalizing a Clarifying Response in a social situation or classroom.

Activity 11

1. Read through some of your old letters from friends or some old term papers or compositions and circle any Value Indicator statements you may come across.

2. Mentally formulate a Clarifying Response for each statement you find.

Activity 12

This activity is designed for use with small groups. Later, you may wish to try it with students.

VALUE CLARIFYING RESPONSE GAME

Player number 1 writes a value statement (I believe _____. I want to be _____.). Player number 2 is designated scorekeeper. Only these two players see the written statement.

All the other players ask questions to seek further information, such as "How did you come to believe this?" "What do you intend to do about it?" "What would you have me do to help?"

Player number 1 answers all questions without disclosing the original statement.

The other players try to guess the values statement. The person guessing it then becomes the next to write a statement and the previous one becomes scorekeeper. (Limit questions to ten or fifteen.)

Activity 13

This activity is designed for use with small groups. Later, you may wish to try it with students.

I HEARD
YOU SAY. . . .

The first player writes a statement on the board and reads it to the group. It can indicate an attitude, an aspiration, a purpose, an interest, an activity, or a feeling.

Each other person writes all of the inferences that he or she can make from that statement. As they are read, the first player responds with "Yes, you heard that" or "No, I didn't say that."

Sample statement: "I want to be an airlines pilot.
Response: "You like to fly."
"You like to travel."
"You like being in control."

Activity 14

This activity is designed to be used with individual students after you've been using the Clarifying Response for a while. It is a technique for helping individuals further analyze the implications of value-related statements they have made.

PLANTING A DREAM

The teacher may distribute this sheet to be filled in. It is a diagram of a seed, above which is a flower and below which is a root system. The seed represents the dream or ambition (goal), the flower represents an extended possibility, and the roots, steps in achieving the goal. Each extension of the root system represents activities which prepare for the next step. Eventually the person is saying "these are things I can do today."

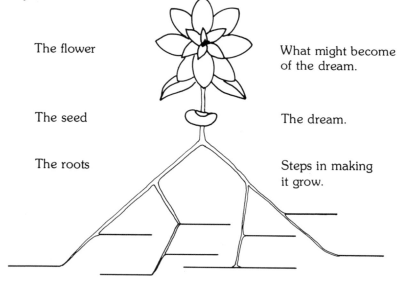

The flower   What might become
                          of the dream.

The seed   The dream.

The roots   Steps in making
                          it grow.

Values Clarification Methods: Discussion Activities

5

Before beginning to read this chapter, view the MEDIAPAK audio-visual components labeled "5 Values Clarification Methods: Discussion Activities."

When you have completed this module, you will be able to:

1. *Identify five values clarification discussion activities.*

2. *Choose a topic and develop "starter" questions for a Value-Clarifying Discussion.*

3. *List some possible situations for values-related Role Playing.*

4. *Describe the use of the Contrived Incident.*

5. *Describe the use of the Zig-Zag lesson.*

6. *Identify possible issues for the Values Continuum.*

7. *Implement at least one of the discussion methods with a group.*

All of the information needed to meet these objectives is presented in MEDIAPAK 5, in Part Three of the text *Values and Teaching*, and in this chapter, where values clarification discussion methods are reviewed and expanded.

MEDIAPAK 5 features an overview of five methods which can be used for promoting classroom discussions on value-related issues and topics. The methods presented are the Value-Clarifying Discussion, Role Playing, the Contrived Incident, the Zig-Zag Lesson, and the Values Continuum.

THE VALUE-CLARIFYING DISCUSSION

The Value-Clarifying Discussion differs from other discussions (teaching or review) in that the teacher does not judge the adequacy of answers, "dispense knowledge," or guide the discussion. The teacher facilitates an open discussion and is *always* accepting of *all* viewpoints. He or she helps students to examine alternatives and consequences and encourages individual choices. Value-Clarifying Discussions can lead to written tasks where students reflect on a topic privately.

Some examples of discussion "starters" are included here. But remember, any topic of general interest to the group as a whole is appropriate.

Example A.   A Value-Clarifying Discussion may be based on a quotation or simple statement.

Man is better off without industries which cause pollution.

Discussion could revolve around such questions as:

What can business do?
What can government do?
What can individuals do?
What can you do?

Example B.   Value-Clarifying Discussions can be directly related to the curriculum, as in this example on the study of Indian cultures and society.

During study of Indian culture, discuss present-day marriage, property ownership, legal responsibilities, and then compare. . .
Women's place—then and now;
Attitudes toward in-laws—then and now;
Time for recreation—then and now.

Ask questions to draw out the students' own opinions.

Example C.   Here is another simple example, evolving from study of the thirteen colonies.

A woman needs only the education necessary for work in the home.

Discussion starter questions could include:

Was this statement true in the days of the Puritans?
Is this statement true today in America?
What role did women play in colonial society?
How has the role of women changed?
How do you feel about the role of women today?

Example D. This example could be used with younger children.

> Can you describe your friends?
>> What things do you do with your friends?
>> Do you like the same games?
>> What do your friends do to make you happy?

Action Projects

There comes a time when talk needs to be turned into action. We can discuss attitudes and write about interests, but our feelings, beliefs, attitudes, and interests are not really closing in on the value level unless we are ready and willing to act on them. Ideas for action projects often evolve out of Value-Clarifying Discussions or written activities. For example, after a study of technological modifications of the ecological system, students could plan how they could modify an empty lot around the community. Or after a unit on conservation of resources students could be given the following assignment:

Find out what people in your community do to conserve one of these resources:

> People
> Air
> Water
> Soil
> Minerals
> Forests

"What could you do to help?" could be the final question, and it would be up to individuals to choose whether or not they want to act upon their interests.

Another example: a class of elementary-school students decided to make planters as gifts for some elderly people at a nearby retirement home and then each student "adopted a Grandparent," whom he or she visited weekly.

ROLE
PLAYING

Role Playing can be an effective tool for eliciting value-related feelings and insights. Younger children can act out fables, fairy tales, and stories and skits and then discuss the feelings and attitudes of the characters. Younger and older students can role play situations coming out of their classroom studies or real-life situations. Here are some examples in addition to those described in *Values and Teaching* and those which will pop up regularly in everyday classroom activities.

1. Role play the younger generation versus the older generation on such topics as:
>   Clothes,
>   Music,
>   Jobs,
>   Free time.

2. Role play situations related to community conflicts such as building a new freeway.
>   Pro: The freeway will make it easier and faster to get to work; property values will rise; etc.
>   Con: We must preserve the rural atmosphere and natural beauty of the community; the taxes will rise; etc.

After the role play is completed, these questions could be raised:

>   a) What are some of the strong points on each side?
>   b) What are some ways this conflict could be resolved?
>   c) What could you do?

3. Younger students could role play feelings such as
    Happy . . . Sad
    Bravery . . . Fear
    Friendliness . . . Hostility

Questions to follow might include:
    Have you ever been in _____ 's position?
    How does it make you feel?

THE CONTRIVED INCIDENT

The Contrived Incident is designed to cut through easy verbalizations and get directly at feelings and real understandings. A discussion always follows. Here are two examples.

1. To demonstrate the concept of inequality:
    All students whose names begin with the first half of the alphabet sit on the floor for the first two hours of school.

2. To demonstrate the value of neatness and the necessity for rules for harmonious and safe living in a group:
    a) All students put their coats in a heap on the floor when they first arrive in the morning.

b) At recess, the teacher excuses all to go and get their coats at the same time.

c) The teacher then asks, "Why did it take so long?" and "What can we do to make it easier and more convenient for us all?"

Think up some more examples of a Contrived Incident or situation that may call for use of a Contrived Incident and list them here.

THE ZIG-ZAG LESSON

The Zig-Zag Lesson is a method of zeroing in on the heart of an issue with one confronting question, after heading up to it with some rather mild and quick questions designed to stimulate interest. Remember Activity 1 in chapter 1—that was an example of the zig-zag approach.

Here is the Zig-Zag Lesson which was in the MEDIAPAK. Notice that the goal of this discussion is to help students appreciate the necessity of following rules for the safety of all, as opposed to merely obeying for fear of punishment. Notice how the last question zeros in on the real issue.

> How do you get to school?
> How many of you walk?
> How many ride in a car?
> How many ride the bus?
> What are some rules you follow on the way to school?
> Suppose there were no rules for stopping at corner signals?

Think up additional examples of a Zig-Zag Lesson and share them with your group.

THE VALUES CONTINUUM

The purpose of the Values Continuum is to visually demonstrate to the class the wide range of possible alternatives for an issue. Two polar positions are listed at opposite ends of a line drawn on the board. Students identify possible alternatives and place them along the continuum.

The example shown in the MEDIAPAK, which was used with a high-school class, was on "The use of energy."

Tight _____Unlimited
conservation   use

Identify three possible issues and the two polar positions, and list them below.

Issue:

_____

Issue:

_____

Issue:

_____

Now try to identify some alternative positions and place these on your continuum lines.

When you have completed this section, turn to the next page and do the *Self-Checking Exercise* for review. Following the Exercise, you'll find some Activities designed to assist you in using Discussion Activities.

SELF-CHECKING EXERCISE

1. The Value-Clarifying Discussion described in this module is another technique for helping students examine their life experiences. This type of discussion has which of the following characteristics:

    a) Occurs after a lecture by the teacher.
    b) Is brief.
    c) Allows students to reflect on an issue.
    d) Is long and complex.

2. Brief discussions on critical issues which allow for independent thinking can be introduced by the teacher. List three "starters" for a Value-Clarifying Discussion.

    a)

    b)

    c)

3. Some starters you might have listed include song lyrics, news editorials, and specific classroom events. The choices are almost endless. In using this technique effectively, the teacher should:

    a) Agree or disagree with each student response.
    b) Be nonjudgmental and accepting.
    c) Try to guide the discussion to a certain conclusion.
    d) Allow students to write about their thoughts afterwards or begin an action project.
    e) Follow the discussion with a short quiz.

4. Value-Clarifying Discussions should be conducted with a minimum of teacher input and direction. Since there is no "right" answer or solution, students feel more free to express themselves openly. Return to the list of discussion starters you made in question **2.** For each idea you listed, briefly describe an *action project* which could be a follow-up to the discussion:

    a)

    b)

    c)

5. Action projects can range from doing something with or for other people to poster campaigns in the school or community. Projects must be freely chosen by the participating students. Now, list some potential outcomes from the action projects you listed above or outcomes from a project you were involved in:

Action project:
Some outcomes:

6. In the second part of MEDIAPAK 5, you learned about four other value-clarifying activities. List them here:

a)

b)

c)

d)

7. Describe a Role Playing situation which would be appropriate to the age and interest level of your students:

8. List some questions you would ask students following the Role Playing session.

9. Role Playing can bring out real feelings and emotions on issues about which students feel strongly. Which of these might the teacher do if a student "gets out of the role" and starts getting into a heated argument?
   a) Allow the student to work it out.
   b) Reverse roles.
   c) Remind the student to "stay in the role."
   d) Stop the activity.
   e) Tell the student what to say.

10. The Contrived Incident and Zig-Zag Lesson are other verbal techniques for values clarification. Choose one of these techniques and describe how you might use it with your students.

11. Can you think of any advantages to these techniques as opposed to written strategies for values clarification? List some.

12. The Values Continuum method is really a combination of verbal and written responses. Describe how you would set up a Values Continuum problem for a group of students.

13. List the subject matter areas in your curriculum that allow the greatest interaction with values-clarification activities.

14. Review your answers to these questions. Have you related values-clarification exercises to your curriculum? Can you think of *more* ways to do this? Revise the activities you designed if you think of new ways to integrate subject matter.

When you have completed this section, turn to the next page and do the Activities. These Activities are designed to provide the opportunity to practice and experience each method before implementing them with students.

VALUE-CLARIFYING DISCUSSION

This activity is designed for use with a group in a college classroom or workshop setting. It can later be tried with students in an upper elementary, junior high, or high school classroom.

Choosing a Topic for Discussion

Each person writes the three topics which interest him or her most. A recorder writes all of these items on the board with a tally, noting those most frequently chosen. Everyone is then given an opportunity to write another list of two topics using the list on the board. These are tallied with the first choices. At this time, two or three of the topics will obviously represent the primary concerns of the class and will elicit the most participation for beginning a discussion.

Write three topics that you are interested in here.

Now proceed to Activity 16 and try out a discussion.

VALUE-CLARIFYING DISCUSSION

Discussion Development

Once a topic of general interest is chosen, the group sits in a circle. Any one person is then asked to make a statement on the topic. Moving to each person in turn around the circle, each has the choice either to repeat a statement previously made, to modify or add to a previous statement, or to say something new that is pertinent to the topic.

As long as the comment relates to the topic, anything is accepted. No comments are allowed from the rest of the group until all have made their original statements. If one person refers to something someone else has said, that person should be mentioned by name.

After going full circle, the topic is open for additional comments.

VALUE-CLARIFYING DISCUSSION

This activity is designed for use with a group in a college classroom or workshop setting. It can later be tried with students in an upper elementary, junior high, or high school classroom.

Issues Discussion

Using the newspaper, TV, radio, or classroom happenings, the students discover interesting items involving conflicting interests (values). An example might be the control of our pet (or human) population.

One student presents a news item with the obvious alternative points of view. During the next five minutes, the group considers choices inherent to the conflict (one or more solutions, or possible noninvolvement). A fifteen-minute discussion follows, and then time is called.

The student who introduced the topic then summarizes by briefly listing the different solutions and their apparent consequences. Anyone who would like to continue the discussion or become further involved writes suggestions and gives them to the original presenter, who then decides on possible further action.

ACTION
PROJECT

This activity may be helpful as a technique to get students thinking about acting on some of their value-related thoughts.

Social Action Toss

Purpose: To consider some alternative behaviors and resulting consequences.

Each member of the class writes a social problem on a card, along with six possible social actions relating to it. The actions are numbered and represented by the sides of a die.

The class is then divided into small groups. The first player draws a card and then rolls the die. According to the number which comes up, he or she reads the social action to be taken. The rest of the group responds with possible reactions to that behavior. Each member takes one turn drawing a card and rolling the die.

Activity 19

ROLE
PLAYING

This activity is designed for use with students in elementary, junior high, or high school classes.

Masks are made of papier maché. The last layer to be applied is a strip from the Sunday comics.

An individual chooses one of the characters from his mask and holds the mask in front of his face. The group become reporters and hold a press conference. The individual responds to current event questions as he thinks his comic strip character would react.

Two or three masks from the same strip can be used for discussions on any current topic, from the viewpoints of the different characters.

Note: This is a safe way to introduce individual differences and acceptance of different points of view.

Activity 20

VALUES
CONTINUUM

Hanging Out the Wash

This is a useful technique when the group is actively involved in controversy.

Have each individual write what he or she feels his or her attitude or solution is. When completed, each person should read that statement to the group, and the group places each written statement on a continuum. The statements can be tacked across the front of the room or actually hung on a clothes line.

This is a concrete method of displaying the many possible positions which can be taken on any one topic.

VALUES
CONTINUUM

This activity is designed for use with an individual student.

The Values Continuum Script

When a person expresses a strong opinion, suggest that he or she write a dialogue with an imaginary other person. Each of them should begin with extreme opposing views; but as the dialogue progresses, each modifies the point of view until they have reached agreement on a middle stance.

When someone seems noncommital, suggest writing a dialogue as before, except begin with the two in agreement but progress to the extreme opposing views.

This completes our chapter on Discussion Methods. At this point, you may wish to take a little break from this program and actually try implementing one or more of these methods with some students.

6

Taking a New Road:
Getting Started—
Keeping Going

Before beginning to read this chapter, view the MEDIAPAK audio-visual component labeled "6, Taking a New Road: Getting Started—Keeping Going."

When you have completed both the media and print portions of this module, you will be able to:

1. *Express how you have dealt with your questions and/or concerns about the use of values clarification methods.*

2. *List seven guidelines for the effective use of values clarification in the school setting.*

3. *Assess whether your attitudes, beliefs, feelings, and values related to students and to providing values education have changed since you began this program.*

4. *Describe the results of the values clarification methods you have tried in terms of the choosing, prizing, and acting behaviors of your students.*

5. *Affirm whether or not values clarification is an effective approach for you, and describe how you are acting as a result of your choice.*

All of the information needed to meet these objectives is presented in MEDIAPAK 6 (which builds on all the preceding modules in this program), in Part Four of the text *Values and Teaching,* and in this chapter, where the seven guidelines for using vaues clarification are discussed.

THE VALUES CLARIFICATION WAY

In the preceding five modules of this program on *Values in the Classroom,* you were introduced to the process of valuing and to a variety of values clarification techniques. You learned how to distinguish between a value and a value indicator, and how to begin to create an optimal environment for values development. You had a chance to assess your own readiness for interacting with students in ways that facilitate values growth. Examples of different values clarification methods were shown, and you were given opportunities to practice and to experiment with these methods. For some of you, the ideas and techniques presented merely reinforced your own thinking and classroom practices. Others of you, perhaps, learned a whole new approach to values education. Probably many of you were somewhere in between these two extremes, and you may have acquired some new techniques or refined the methods you were already using. In any event, this program was designed to guide you in clarifying your *own* approach to values education. If you followed the suggestion made earlier, and kept notes on any questions or concerns that came to mind as you studied this program and as you tried the methods for yourself and with students, you might wish to look over those notes now, before you read the following section.

You Were Asking?

1. *"Aren't there some basic values—like honesty, for instance—that ought to be taught to all children?"* This question reveals something about what is of value to the person asking it; and that is very important, because public affirmation is one of the characteristics of valuing. What is also important is whether this person freely chose honesty as a value for himself or herself and whether this person actually lives in accordance with this value. You see, we can "teach" students many facts, many concepts, many "values," but what they learn—what is powerful enough to actually guide and shape their lives—is *self-taught*. It is learned through a process of selecting, analyzing, deciding, reflecting, and evaluating for *oneself*. The issue is not which values to teach, but rather, which *methods* can help students to develop values of their own.

2. *"Well, honesty is one of my values, and I think I should express this, and other values, to my students, but will this interfere with my being an effective facilitator?"* As we said, affirming and acting on your values is

basic to the whole process of valuing. As a person and as a teacher-facilitator, you should definitely be open and forthright about your own values. This does not mean, however, that you should try to impose your value structure on others. Moralizing, acting "holier-than-thou," and coercing are usually inappropriate behaviors for a facilitator of *any* type of meaningful learning. In the area of values, such behaviors are actually contradictory to the meaning and the essence of valuing. *Do* take a stand, but let your position on a values issue be seen by your students as one alternative among several, not as the "ultimate" or "only" acceptable view. Participate in values clarification activities with your students, but take your turn last. Of course, you may choose to reject this point of view, just as you are free to choose to reject all or any part of our approach to values education!

Now, if you're still with us, let's look at a third concern that many teachers have about using values clarification.

3.   *"Does allowing freedom of choice mean that I have to accept any kind of behavior from my students, no matter how much it bothers me?"* Absolutely not! Values acquisition, like most other types of learning in group settings, takes place best when there are some parameters, or even rules. We are certainly not advocating that teachers relinquish their authority and responsibility as adults. There are certain behaviors which cannot be tolerated in a classroom. Within the range of what is acceptable group or social behavior in the school, there are some teachers who can tolerate more divergence, variety, and individuality than others. Young children need limits for their own protection; older students need some

stability, structure, and guidance so that they can get on with the business of learning. These statements are more or less generally accepted facts about learning and development, and the values clarification approach is designed to take these facts into account. You can set some limits and establish general guidelines for student behavior and still convey respect for individuals by acknowledging that outside of school, in other areas of their lives, they may choose to act different. The important thing is to be open and consistent about the limits and guidelines you create, as well as willing to reveal your rationale for creating them. Be aware of your own needs and values.

4. *"How can I help my students clarify their values when I'm still working on clarifying my own?"* Persons who ask this question probe deeply at the heart of our view of valuing, for we see it as a life-long process. Values are not static; they are continually evolving and changing—sometimes dramatically and sometimes imperceptibly—in response to life itself. Adults who cope effectively and joyfully with life usually are operating from a certain framework, or core, of values which they can see and articulate clearly. However, as these persons strive to actualize more and more of their human potential, there are from time to time areas of thinking and feeling which are fuzzy or as yet undefined. This is especially true of people who have learned to intuitively use the process of valuing described here. Working on clarifying your values is, in fact, a desirable space to be in. And if that's where you find yourself, you will likely be much more able to help students clarify *their* values than will

the person who has found the "answers" and thereafter stopped growing. If you are willing to let students know about values that you are trying
to clarify for yourself, you will be maximally effective as a facilitator, since
you will actually be modelling the process of valuing. Furthermore, your
openness and frankness will make it possible for your students to respect
you for being *you,* for being who you are.

At this point, we'd like to suggest to those of you who found, as a result
of completing the rating scale in chapter 2, that you wanted to develop
some new outlooks and skills, to take a few moments right now to
complete the same rating scale again. This exercise will enable you to
assess whether or not your attitudes, beliefs, and values have changed,
and if so in what ways, since you began this program. Do you now
possess, to some degree, all twenty characteristics of an effective
facilitator of values development? Those of you who do not wish to
reassess your personal assets as a values facilitator may turn directly to
page 101.

Activity 22

Rating Scale for Teacher-Facilitators of Values Education

Directions: Write today's date here_____and
rank yourself, as of *this* point in time, on all of the following variables:

	1 hardly ever	2 sometimes	3 often	4 almost always
1. I act as though I believe students are capable of self-directed learning.				
2. When I meet students for the first time, I look for the uniqueness in each one.				
3. I seek ways to enhance both cognitive *and* affective development in students.				
4. I take responsibility for trying to help meet some of the emotional needs of students I work with.				
5. I grow and learn through my interactions with the people around me.				
6. I try to get to know students as persons.				
7. I take time to examine *my* personal feelings, attitudes, values.				
8. I am clear about certain values of my own.				
9. I am working on clarifying some of my own values.				
10. I attempt to guide rather than direct student learning, and I let students think for themselves.				
11. I make alternative tasks, activities, responses available to students.				
12. I encourage students to suggest their own alternatives.				
13. I allow freedom of choice among the available alternatives.				
14. I encourage and assist students to weigh their choices and to consider possible consequences of their actions both in and outside the classroom.				

	1 hardly ever	2 sometimes	3 often	4 almost always
15. I ask students questions about what is important to them, what they prize in life.				
16. I encourage students to examine their beliefs, attitudes, feelings for meaning.				
17. I allow students to verbally express their opinions, convictions, and values and support them in doing so.				
18. I try to listen and hear what students are saying in their words and actions.				
19. I define the classroom structure and limits I feel to be essential.				
20. I respect the lives and rights of students.				

Compare your responses to those you made the first time (Chapter 2).

BEGINNING AND CONTINUING AS A VALUES FACILITATOR

In MEDIAPAK 6 we listed seven guidelines to assist you in using the values clarification methods (modules 3, 4, and 5) effectively. We now conclude this program on *Values in the Classroom* by expanding upon these guidelines.

1. Create a Psychologically Safe Environment

Now that you have had an opportunity to become familiar with values clarification methods, by completing the activities in this book and using similar activities with students, you probably have a clearer understanding of why we have underscored this guideline throughout the program. Only in an environment where there is *mutual* trust and respect can students dare to risk, to become involved, to the extent necessary if they are to develop personal values. Acquiring and acting upon your personal values involves the risk of self-disclosure—a risk that can be taken in stride when you feel that others regard you as important and unique.

An atmosphere in which students are encouraged and helped to reflect on what choices they have made, what they have learned, how their learning affects their lives, and what they need to learn next is necessary for values development. To attempt to use values clarification activities in any other kind of environment will dilute the potential effects of the method, or even entirely negate the process of valuing.

2. Provide Structure for Values Development

Just as most responsible educators would argue that math, civics, or geography can best be learned in a classroom full of learning ideas and materials which are used within some inherent structure, we suggest that values education is most effective when the teacher carefully plans for it. The process of valuing is too important to leave to chance, and therefore it is essential to prepare materials, organize time, and provide clear directions for values-related activities. The intimate relationship of the process of valuing to all areas of the curriculum has been illustrated in the three preceding modules. Meaningful learning is experiential. So is valuing; therefore, it is not desirable, or even possible, to separate values education from other areas of teaching and learning. Behaviors which will determine your students' futures will, however, be learned by *them*, directly or indirectly, regardless of what methods you as a teacher use.

What we have been emphasizing in this program is an approach to ensure that the behaviors acquired by your students are those which will best serve *each* of them individually as they make their way through life. By providing an optimal atmosphere and the essential structure for personal growth experiences, teachers can help students acquire and live the values that let them become effective, happy, growing persons.

3.   Avoid Moralizing

Convincing others to do something or to believe in something may be very appropriate in certain circumstances. Actors, preachers, and sales-people make it a way of life. In teaching there is often an almost "natural" tendency to use persuasion of various sorts, ranging from gentle prompts to outright threats, to get students to do certain things. Granted, there are situations when drastic tactics may be necessary—particularly where there is physical danger. Valuing, however, is not that kind of situation, and to use methods such as preaching, nagging, or arguing to get another person to accept your point of view on a values-related issue denies that person his or her right to think, feel, act for himself. A "value" which is not chosen freely and prized dearly, is not, in our view, a value at all.

4.   Introduce Values Clarification Gradually

You have recently been exposed to a wide variety of values clarification methods and activities. These were presented in a particular sequence, beginning with methods that are usually easiest to use and which require the least self-disclosure. To be effective as a facilitator of values develop-ment, you will need to select one or two methods which you wish to begin

using with your students. Then you will need to analyze the results of these methods carefully, taking care to evaluate the *methods* and not the *students,* to determine their usefulness. Gradually move on to another method when you and your students feel ready. Compare the effects of different methods. Ask the students what is most helpful to them. Remember—behavior changes slowly; your students should be given a chance to become comfortable with the whole idea of developing and clarifying values. They must also be allowed to decide for themselves when they are ready to participate in values clarification activities. With young children, repeated practice in a particular activity will often be necessary.

5.   Make the Activities Your Own

All the methods, together with the examples presented, are intended merely to get you started successfully as a facilitator. Hopefully, you will have already thought of, or even tried, some activities that are more interesting, more fun, or more relevant for your classroom than the ones in this book. You may have seen ways to adapt or modify some of our activities to make them more meaningful for your students. You may have found that some exercises did not appeal to you. All this is as it should be, for if you are really in tune with what we have been saying about valuing, you will recognize that the methods you use must be *yours.* For this reason, we have included only a small sampling of activities in this book. Our intent was to provide you with a rationale, a structure, and a format for designing values clarification activities. You must relate your own thoughts and feelings, and those of your students, to that structure. Reshape it until it is your own.

6.   Inform Others about Your Use of Values Clarification Activities with Students

Since values and valuing are very personal, there are many different views on values education. It is often helpful to keep parents and other teachers aware of what you are doing in values education. Invite others to read about the approach if they are curious, or to discuss it with you. Be sure to reassure them that students may choose to participate or not in activities calling for self-disclosure.

7.   Be Cautious

We hope that by now you are very excited about the possibilities of using values clarification techniques. Many teachers have already used our methods and have found that their students grow in very positive ways as individuals. In your enthusiasm, however, don't expect miracles. And don't look to values clarification to be the answer to all the problems you may encounter in teaching. Some students may require other kinds of help before they are able to benefit from values clarification, and all students will need time to grow.

Activity 23

This is the last activity in this book. It is very unstructured and very personal. We'd simply like to give you a space to write a few words, or to express in drawing, or in verse, whatever you feel has happened to you, and to those around you, as a result of using the process of valuing. . . .

SOME THOUGHTS AND FEELINGS
WE'D LIKE TO LEAVE WITH YOU

In this concluding chapter of *Values in the Classroom,* we've tried to be very candid with you about the use of values clarification. Throughout the entire program our values have been showing. We believe in the capacity and the right of each individual to express his or her humanity uniquely. We believe values clarification, when used with concern, and care, and love, can be a way of maximizing human potential. We feel joy and hope in sharing our thoughts with you; we invite you to share in our feeling.

References and Suggested Readings

INTRODUCTION
REFERENCES

Raths, Louis, Harmin, Merrill, and Simon, Sidney B. *Values and Teaching.*
    Columbus, Ohio: Charles E. Merrill, 1966.

Simon, Sidney B., Howe, L. W., and Kirschenbaum, H. *Values Clarification:
    A Handbook of Practical Strategies for Teachers and Students,* New York:
    Hart, 1972.

CHAPTER 1
REFERENCES

Ausubel, D. P., and Robinson, F. G. *School Learning: An Introduction to
    Educational Psychology.* New York: Holt, Rinehart and Winston, 1969.

Coombs, A. W. "What Can Man Become?" *California Journal for Supervision
    and Curriculum Development,* **4,** 1961, 15-28.

Hamachek, D. E. *Encounters with the Self.* New York: Holt, Rinehart and
    Winston, 1971.

CHAPTER 2
REFERENCES

Peters, R. S. *Ethics and Education*. Glenview, Ill.: Scott, Foresman, 1967.

Rogers, C. R. *Freedom to Learn*. Columbus, Ohio: Charles E. Merrill, 1969.

Romey, W. D. *Risk—Trust—Love: Learning in a Humane Environment*. Columbus, Ohio: Charles E. Merrill, 1972.

Watts, A. W. *The Book: On the Taboo Against Knowing Who You Are*. New York: Pantheon Books, Random House, 1966.

CHAPTER 4
REFERENCES

Cunningham, R. T. "Developing Question-Asking Skills." In James E. Weigand, ed., *Developing Teacher Competencies*. Englewood Cliffs, N.J.: Prentice-Hall, 1971. Pp. 81-130.

CHAPTER 5
REFERENCES

Center for the Study of Instruction. *Principles and Practices in the Teaching of the Social Sciences: Concepts and Values*. New York: Harcourt, Brace, Jovanovich, 1970.

Curwin, R. L., and Curwin, G. *Developing Individual Values in the Classroom*. Palo Alto, Calif.: Learning Handbooks, 1974.

Gillespie, M. C., and Thompson, A. G. *Social Studies in a Multi-Ethnic Society*. Columbus, Ohio: Charles E. Merrill, 1973.

Harmin, M., Kirschenbaum, H., and Simon, S. *Clarifying Values through Subject Matter: Applications for the Classroom*. Minneapolis, Winston Press, 1973.

SUGGESTED
READINGS

Casteel, J. D., and Stahl, R. J. *Value Clarification in the Classroom: A Primer*. Pacific Palisades, Calif.: Goodyear Publishing, 1975.

Colby, A. "Book Review of Raths, L.E., Harmin, M., and Simon, S.B., *Values and Teaching.* Columbus, Ohio: Charles E. Merrill, 1966, and Simon, S.B., Howe, L.W., and Kirschenbaum, H. *Values Clarification: A Handbook of Practical Strategies for Teachers and Students.* New York: Hart, 1972." *Harvard Educational Review,* **45,** 1975, 134-43.

Curwin, R. L., and Curwin, G. "Building Trust: A Starting Point for Clarifying Values." *Learning,* **3** (6), 1975, 30-36.

Gray, F. "Doing Something About Values," *Learning,* **1** (2), 1972, 15-18.

Knicker, C. R. *You and Values Education.* Columbus, Ohio: Charles E. Merrill, 1977.

Kohlberg, L. "The Cognitive-Development Approach to Moral Education."*Phi Delta Kappan,* **56** (10), 1975, 670-77.

Kohlberg, L., and Whitten, P. "Understanding the Hidden Curriculum." *Learning,* **1** (2), 1972, 10-14.

Kurpuis, D. "Developing Teacher Competencies in Interpersonal Transactions." In James E. Weigand, ed., *Developing Teacher Competencies.* Englewood Cliffs, N.J.: Prentice-Hall, 1971. Pp. 246-305.

Phi Delta Kappan, "A Special Issue on Moral Education." **56** (10), 1975, 658-711.

Raths, L. E. *Meeting the Needs of Children: Creating Trust and Security.* Columbus, Ohio: Charles E. Merrill, 1972.